MOLLY KOOL

MOLLY KOOL

CAPTAIN OF THE ATLANTIC

CHRISTINE WELLDON

NIMBUS

PUBLISHING LTD

For my two Miriams, safe harbour in a storm

"Look at that sea, girls—all silver and shadow and vision of things not seen."—Lucy Maud Montgomery

Nimbus Publishing Limited
3731 Mackintosh St, Halifax, NS B3K 5A5
(902) 455-4286 nimbus.ca

Printed and bound in Canada

Author photo: Diana Dines
Design: Jenn Embree

Library and Archives Canada Cataloguing in Publication

Welldon, Christine
        Molly Kool : captain of the Atlantic / Christine Welldon.
        (Stories of our past)
        Includes bibliographical references.
        ISBN 978-1-55109-836-4

1. Kool, Molly, 1916-2009. 2. Women ship captains—New Brunswick—Biography. 3. Seafaring life—Fundy, Bay of. I. Title. II. Series: Stories of our past (Halifax, N.S.)

VK140.K66W45 2011   387.5092   C2011-900033-4

Nimbus Publishing acknowledges the financial support for its publishing activities from the Government of Canada through the Canada Book Fund (CBF) and the Canada Council for the Arts, and from the Province of Nova Scotia through the Department of Communities, Culture and Heritage.

TABLE OF CONTENTS

Molly Kool was to prove over and over again that she was just as good as any man.

MAN OVERBOARD!

Fog drifted over the water, with not a breath of wind to stir it. The scow, *Jean K*, had just loaded lumber in Point Wolfe and was running in to Saint John. The captain of the *Jean K*, peering through the mist and dead reckoning their location, could see the vague outline of a channel-marker buoy. There was barely time to register the uneasy sense that another vessel was close, when from out of the fog came the blood-chilling sound of a horn. A steamship was fast bearing down on the *Jean K*. As a grinding, shivering jolt shook the scow, and the sound of timbers tearing and splintering filled the air, the captain was knocked overboard.

"Man overboard!" yelled the crew, leaning over the rails to search for their skipper and hurling anything that would float. Passengers on the steamer heaved life rings overboard, but the captain had already grabbed some planks that had fallen off the deck.

"Stop throwing this rubbish on me," she yelled, ignoring the life rings. "I'm already floating!"

The captain was a woman, and her name was Molly Kool.

It was the year 1939, when women who worked on ships were considered bad luck to the crew, and captaining

"They're throwing life rings at me....I knew I was pretty safe with those two planks under my arm, and I'm ducking those damn things."

ships was strictly for men. But Captain Kool was to prove over and over that she was just as capable as any man.

"I went over on the starboard side and came out on the port side," said Captain Kool, in her account of the accident.

> Oh, I was drifting down by the Boston boat and they're throwing those life rings at me. Well, I knew I was pretty safe with those two planks under my arm. And I'm ducking those damn things. Well, that's the way it went. I sure wasn't familiar with a life ring. And some fishermen was there and I had grabbed a couple of planks under each arm. And the fishermen picked me up. And I know that we got a tugboat somehow, someway. And it come in and towed the *Jean K* in. But it had taken the cabin partially off so that we had to rebuild the cabin on her.

Captain Kool and friend on the *Jean K.*

In 1939, the year that Canada declared war on Germany, air-conditioned cars were introduced, and women's skirts were raised to a length no higher than their knees, Molly Kool became the first female sea captain to command a ship in North America. She was a woman who would fire the imagination of future generations, and overcome entrenched prejudices about gender. She was known for saying, "You think I can't do it? Just watch me!"

CHAPTER ONE

SUPERSTITION AND CONDESCENSION

IF A QUEBEC fisherman saw a woman before he boarded his boat, he returned home, took holy water, and repeatedly recited the "Hail Mary." In Scotland, the timbers for a new boat were chosen carefully, because "male" timbers would help the ship sail faster during the day. In Sweden, it was unlucky if a woman asked a fisherman where he was going while he was heading for his boat. Women in England could not even step over a fishing line for fear of causing a disaster at sea. It is no surprise that superstitions about women and the sea have endured through the ages, but somewhat puzzling that the ship itself remains feminine, as Joseph Conrad reminded us in his book, *Mirror of the Sea*:

> Your ship is a tender creature, whose idiosyncrasies must be attended to if you mean her to come with credit to herself and you through the rough and tumble of life…those sensitive creatures have no ears for blandishments. It takes something more than mere words to cajole them to do our will, to cover us with glory.[1]

Opposite page: Captain Molly Kool

An artist's rendition of Captain Kool, age 23.

time who usually became teachers or nurses, worked until they married, and stayed home to raise their families.

A newspaper interview with Molly Kool in 1939 shows exactly what she was up against. The reporter introduced the interview with Molly this way:

Amidst this jumble of superstition, prejudice, and stark fear, was the belief that women were incompetent in a man's world and could not be trusted to learn seafaring skills. During the age of sail, and later of steam, ships were always male-dominated workplaces, and only rarely was a woman hired to work on board. Ruling the seas was the birthright of men for thousands of years, and at the very least women were expected to stay away from the engine room and bridge. There were few jobs to be had at sea, and any added competition was a threat to men's livelihoods. Seafaring also represented an escape from women and the demands of home life. Women belonged in the home, and should stay there. One seaman, when questioned on this topic, said, "My wife didn't work. I didn't want her to. I said it was up to me. I'd like to think that when I come home, I got a wife to be able to talk to, and I figured, it's up to me to support you, if I ask you to marry me."[?]

In 1939, the year that Molly—at twenty-three years of age—was captaining her own ship, a few women, around 2 percent of workers all together, were cooks or stewardesses working in the galleys of passenger steamships, or performing cleaning and laundering duties. They were kept apart from deckhands, and their costume was black rubber-soled shoes, plain grey stockings, and skirts with hems that rose no higher than twenty-five centimetres above the ground. Even short sleeves were forbidden. While it is true that some jobs required physical strength, most jobs could have been done by women if they had been given equal opportunities. Molly was proof of this, but she was considered an oddity among women of the

Always fun-loving, Molly (left) poses with family in Alma, NB

What would those hard-boiled old shipmasters, who commanded vessels out of this very spot, say to a girl being called "captain" and holding a master's ticket! I think I can feel a blueness in the

The Seafaring Maiden of Granville

Elizabeth Pritchard Hall of Granville Ferry, nick-
named "The Seafaring Maiden of Granville," is
believed to be the first woman to captain a
ship across the Atlantic Ocean. Elizabeth's
father, Captain Hall, was part owner of the vessel
Rothesay and was preparing to leave New Orleans
for Liverpool with a cargo of cotton. After a
long layover in port, many of the crew deserted.
Undaunted, and with a crew of only six men, the
first mate, and the ship's carpenter, Captain Hall
set sail anyway.

As the ship rounded the tip of Florida and
entered the Gulf Stream, the first mate and captain
both came down with smallpox. Before taking
to his bunk, Captain Hall appointed Elizabeth
the captain and promoted the seventy-two-year-
old carpenter to first mate. With the help of the
remaining crew, "Captain Bessie" spent the next
twelve days navigating through a storm between
Florida and Newfoundland. In addition to acting as captain, Bessie stood a regular watch from
eight o'clock at night until two in the morning.
Although given up for lost, the ship arrived in
Liverpool. It had taken forty-nine days to make a
crossing that could usually be completed in thirty.

air and hear the angry thump of sea boots on the
quarterdeck, even from their ghosts.

"Molly," said I, "suppose you were married—are
you going to get married?'"

"Maybe," says Molly.

"Well, suppose you were married and your husband was first mate on the vessel you commanded?" I asked.

"I'd make him toe the mark."

"Suppose now, he was captain and you were first mate?"

"I'd do everything he told me," said Molly firmly, "that pertained to the running of the ship."

"Can you cook, Molly?"

"Sure, I can cook, but I don't do much cooking on the boat. I have to sail her."[3]

In a separate interview, Molly had this to say when she was asked who did the cooking on board.

"Who did the cooking? Me. I ran the engines, I pumped the bilges, I'd heave the anchor, I hoisted the sail. The cooking was a disaster. That wasn't too good. When I first went we had an old guy that had been doing the cooking. His name was Alec Brewster and he was telling me how to cook, because we made our own breads. But I was going to make some chicken and rice soup. Well, I put a whole package of rice in the soup. Well, I had enough rice to fill the Bay of Fundy. But then I learned to cook a little bit after awhile. Well, everybody lived anyway. I didn't poison anybody."

The gender divide was not easy to cross, but at a time when women were fighting for the right to be considered as persons, Captain Kool had already crossed it and achieved her own liberation. How did she do it? Many decades later, after a lifetime of adventures, Molly tried

to answer this question: "I was proud, but no more than any man would be. This had nothing to do with women's liberation or anything. I had always thought like a man anyway, and I was only thinking about making a living."

Molly's favourite view of Alma.

CHAPTER TWO
GROWING UP FEMALE

MOLLY'S BIRTHPLACE, the town of Alma, New Brunswick, sits on the Bay of Fundy at the entrance to Fundy National Park where conifer hills meet the waters of the Bay of Fundy. Here, the highest tides in the world can achieve a height of nine metres along the shoreline. As the huge tides move icy water in and out of the bay, warm water meets cold and creates thick fog. When the wind blows, the water is whipped into unruly waves. It was on these challenging waters that young Molly sailed with her father.

"When you get up at the upper end of the bay, the tides are forty feet. The harbour goes dry for two or three miles, and when you went out from that harbour, you were out until the next tide came in," she recalled. At the tender age of five, during her first trip with her father to Apple River, Molly became so ill that her father took her ashore. It was the first time that Molly was ever seasick—and it never happened again. She had found her sea legs, and her calling, early in life.

Alma, a historic settlement, and birthplace of Molly Kool.

Alma

The town of Alma, once named the Salmon River Settlement, began with the construction of a sawmill for the lumber trade on the Upper Salmon River. The parish of Alma was created in 1856, to commemorate the recent Battle of Alma during the Crimean War. In 1948, the federal government expropriated land in the village and surrounding area for the creation of Fundy National Park and many homes were relocated east of the Salmon River. In 1966, the village became an incorporated municipality. A monument on the waterfront marks Molly Kool's accomplishments.

In 1921, when five-year-old Molly was taking this first voyage, women from other regions had abandoned their corsets, bobbed their hair, and dramatically shortened their skirts. It was a time of new beginnings for women, this decade between the two world wars. The flappers— modern young women who went on dates without a chaperone, wore fashionable clothes and makeup, and often had jobs—were drawn to new opportunities. However, sons were still preferred to daughters, the masculine pronoun was the most commonly used, and marriage was a girl's true destiny.

Girls were encouraged to look pretty and invite boys' attention by hiding any smarts they might possess. They collected homemaking badges in Girl Guides, and were taught a "family life" program in Canadian Girls in Training (CGIT), a church-based group that provided leadership training for young women. High schools offered domestic science and commercial classes for girls, while boys were welcomed into math, science, and shop classes. This ensured that if girls entered the workforce prior to marriage, it was to take jobs that would not compete with the employment of men.

Women growing up in the interwar years helped add to the family income by sewing or babysitting at home, or becoming factory workers or sales clerks. Among the small numbers of women who attended university, the majority enrolled in education, nursing, and household science courses. These women found work as teachers or nurses, but any work ended with marriage. Women were regularly passed over for advancement, but the rising tide of feminism pointed out these inequities. The existing federal law stated, "Women are persons in matters of pains and penalties, but are not persons in matters of rights and privileges."

In 1908, a bill in New Brunswick to grant full suffrage to white women was defeated, although a municipal franchise was eventually given to married women. In 1919, the year of Molly's birth, New Brunswick at last joined other provinces by granting everyone the right

The Persons Case

Known as the Famous Five, they were Emily Murphy, Henrietta Muir Edwards, Nellie McClung, Louise McKinney, and Irene Parlby. Nellie McClung took on numerous roles throughout her lifetime. A teacher, temperance leader, suffragist, lecturer, politician, historian, wife, mother, and activist, McClung was also a famous writer, authoring numerous essays and articles, and fifteen books. An active journalist and founder of several clubs, she was the Liberal member of the Alberta legislature for Edmonton from 1921 to 1926.

to vote regardless of race, colour, or sex. As for women entering politics, in 1928, the Supreme Court of Canada ruled that women, children, and the insane were not persons, and could not sit in the Canadian Senate. Years earlier, an attorney general for New Brunswick had stated that he had too much respect for women to wish to see them "dragged from the height upon which [they] stood and brought into the arena of politics."

Five Alberta women challenged the legal definition of "person" and demanded the right to be recognized as "full persons" and consequently, the right to enter politics. They won this right for Canadian women in 1929, with the aptly named "Persons Case." However, whenever the word "person" was used in the changed text of the British North America Act, a masculine pronoun was sure to follow.

This awareness of rising feminism and self-fulfillment for women hardly existed in rural New Brunswick,

The feminist movement hardly existed in the sheltered village of Alma.

and certainly not in Alma, where Molly grew up. The little village on the banks of the Bay of Fundy was co-cooned from such explosive influences. Even so, among the families in Alma who owned farms or operated their own vessels, it was not unusual to see girls and women working alongside men, performing "man's work."

Alma was a sawmill town, but by the late 1800s, the easily accessible trees had been decimated, and sawmill refuse had clogged rivers and harmed fish populations. Land jobs in the village were seasonal. In winter, there was work to be found in the lumber camps and on the spring log drives, but the fishing began to decline, as it suffered from falling prices and a plunging economy.

A Proud Heritage

The connection between New Brunswickers and
their forest heritage began many centuries ago.
Early First Nations people relied on the forest for
food, clothing, and shelter. They developed spiritual
traditions based on trees, and gathered woodland
plants for medicine. European pioneers used wood
to make tools, to build their homes, and for fuel.
Forestry, including pulp and paper, is still the largest
industry in New Brunswick today. The first wood
pulp mills opened in the late 1800s at Penobsquis in
Kings County and Miramichi. There were over three
hundred sawmills in New Brunswick at the peak of
the logging industry between 1810 and 1840. Mills
were always located near a river as this was the only
means of transporting the lumber. The logs were
dumped in the water in the spring and gathered at a
booming area for sorting.

Sawmill owner Judson Arthur Cleveland was possibly
the most outstanding citizen of Alma for his role in
holding the community in place; his sawmill continued
to run despite the bad economic times, providing livelihoods so that families might remain in the area.

The Maritimes didn't experience the Roaring
Twenties and that decade's economic prosperity. By
1922, the large mills, river drives, and shipbuilding
were no more. Manufacturing declined dramatically in
the region, causing considerable hardship. The Great
Depression of the 1930s led to a worsening of already
difficult times. Many people migrated, seeking better opportunities in cities elsewhere in Canada and the United

The Square-Rigger

Square-rigged vessels have all the sails on one or more masts set from yards, wooden spars attached perpendicularly to the masts. Sails were square or rectangular in shape, giving the rig its name. These vessels could, and usually did, carry some triangular jibs and/or staysails between the foremast and bowsprit.

States. But some stayed, possessing the drive and skills to make ends meet in a declining economy.

Molly's father, Paul Kool, was born near Rotterdam, on a Dutch coastal vessel that sailed on the Zuiderzee and other canals of Holland. The son of a Dutch square-rigger master, Paul was orphaned in his early years. He lived in an orphanage until he was twelve, then joined the Dutch Royal Navy and worked on merchant vessels. At the age of eighteen, he and some fellow crew members jumped ship in an Australian port. Paul Kool joined a square-rigged merchant ship that brought him across the ocean to the shores of New Brunswick. Here, the C. T. White Company was hiring crews for its lumber scows, which operated out of Alma. Paul Kool officially applied for Canadian immigrant status, and in 1912, he took a job in Alma as port captain. During World War One, he worked on the scows and built schooners for the White firm. The call of the sea was a strong influence, and he soon began to captain a scow named the *Riverside*, hauling gravel and sand for the Blakeny firm in Moncton during the summer months. In the winter his freight was lumber, cement, and Christmas trees.

Paul Kool was a pioneer in winter scowing, as it was

Molly's family home, preserved today, was built by United Empire Loyalists. Molly always spoke fondly of Alma and of the little house at the head of the mill pond.

customary for the scows to operate only from early spring to late fall. Winter storms did not faze him as he hauled freight from the Albert County shore to Saint John. In those days, the scow captains rarely had formal licenses, but earned their rank by simply keeping themselves and their crews out of harm's way. Most of the scows had one large mainsail along with a gasoline or diesel engine. Their captains and crew hailed from either the French shore on one side of the Petitcodiac River, or from the English shore, on the other. The crews from either side were sociable when they met in the ports and other places around the Fundy shore.

Paul Kool met and married Myrtle Anderson, a local Alma woman. He was soon supervising a fleet of wooden barges that ferried lumber to the large ships at sea. Paul and Myrtle had a large family of five children but two of Molly's siblings died shortly after birth due to a whooping cough epidemic; the vaccine for the disease had not yet been invented. One of Paul Kool's log entries at the time states poignantly, "Didn't work today because my baby died."[4]

The village of Alma was nestled on the shore with thick woods behind. There were no medical facilities close by and in winter, routes into the village were accessible only by horse and cart or sleigh when they weren't closed by snowfalls. Molly remembered the one narrow cow path that led out through Penobsquis and was not passable until June. There was no convenient highway system with eighteen-wheeler trucks to carry freight. The little villages along the bay and their lumber camps depended on small freighters to survive. Freighters would haul in raw materials and haul out the end product— the processed lumber. Molly felt that her father actually began the industry of hauling lumber. He saw the need and followed through, spurring on others to do the same.

The Weir

The fish weir is a method of catching fish that dates back thousands of years. It is constructed by placing stakes in the middle of a stream, in an estuary, or near a coastline. Plant material is then wrapped around and between the stakes and the fish are herded into this circle where they can be easily caught.

Molly had great respect for her father: "He was a very smart man, and very well liked. And he earned it! He was a hard-working man, very faithful to his family, and very honest."

Her older sister Jean was also on board, along with their brother John. Molly had many months of experience before she started full-time on the sea, because she always went with her dad in the summertime during school vacation. She was put to work like any other crew member, despite her age and size. She learned to steer when she could barely see over the wheel by standing on a box and receiving instructions from her father. Sanitation on board was not up to standard, and the men completed their toilet functions over the rail. When Molly or Jean were aboard, their toilet was a bucket placed below deck.

For the crewmen Paul hired, the pay was thirty dollars per month and whatever food they ate on board. Paul's monthly earnings never exceeded four hundred dollars. After skippering a number of the Blakeny scows, Paul began building his own scow in the fall of 1929. He designed it differently than the others. Its shape was less box-like because the flat bottom was twelve metres long,

Little Molly and older sister Jean with the family pets.

Little villages and their lumber camps along the river depended on scows and small freighters to survive.

much shorter than the twenty-one-metre deck. Planks of fir made up its sides, and native spruce and hardwood were used for the decks and bottom respectively. Initially, scows had sails and no motors, but Kool wanted his scow

to have both. He christened the scow the *Jean K*, after his eldest daughter.

The family cottage was situated in a good place for boat building as it faced a breakwater and backed onto a forest. Paul and his crew built the scow using the spruce and fir that were so plentiful near the home. Thirty-five

The River that Bends and Turns

The Petitcodiac River runs through land that was occupied by the Mi'kmaq and Maliseet First Nations. The name *Petitcodiac* is believed to derive from *Pet-kot-que*, which means "the river that bends and turns," or "the river that bends around like a bow." The first settlement of Petitcodiac Village started about three kilometres downstream from the present-day location of the village at a portage that linked the Canaan and Petitcodiac rivers. A portage is an area of land between two waterways over which travellers carry their canoes to avoid obstacles such as rapids, or to transfer from one waterway to another. The portage linking the Canaan and the Petitcodiac was used by the Maliseet and Mi'kmaq, and most likely by early French and English settlers.

centimetre Douglas fir were split down the middle to make eighteen-centimetre sides that were strong enough to bear weight. In those days, ships were built using a supporting piece of timber set at a right angle. The roots of tall trees, called "knees," were useful as they helped provide the support needed to secure parts of the ship together. The forward side of the ship's beam was secured to the ship's side and then the aft of the beam to the ship's side, offering a natural form that shaped the backbone of the ship. Paul hired lumber crews that went in and chopped down trees for this purpose.

During his scow's maiden voyage hauling lumber up the coast, there were not enough funds to install an engine or mast, so the scow had only the bare necessities.

Molly knew the landscape like the back of her hand and didn't often need to check the compass bearings.

Paul Kool planned to add other items as he earned the money needed to do so. On its first short run to Herring Cove, the scow was towed by a tugboat, and as soon as his crew unloaded the lumber and there were more funds available, Paul purchased an engine. Then it was on to Martin Head, where he picked up an anchor and chain and another load of lumber for Saint John. There, a second engine was added and after the next voyage, a mast and sail were installed.

Paul Kool would often sail to Grand Manan with young Molly to load weir poles and brush, used for weir fishing. Molly recalled that the weir poles were long hardwood poles—some of them as long as eighteen metres—used as stakes to build the weir. The stakes were placed in a circle and tied with brush to create a dark place that would attract the fish, making them easy to catch.

Molly always spoke fondly of Alma, and the little house at the head of the millpond where she had a view of the mill from her window. Later, Molly and her family moved into one of the mill houses nearer to the village. A spark from the mill caused a fire that almost destroyed Alma, and the family moved into the home that is preserved today, an historic house built by the United Empire Loyalists.

Molly could play sports as well as any boy, although there were no organized games, such as hockey or baseball, where she could test her mettle. She and her friends skated on the lake in the winter and learned to swim there in the summer. Molly was an excellent swimmer, often diving off tall piles of lumber into the harbour with her friends. On warm summer days, the swimming hole that formed at low tide was the neighbourhood gathering place. The cowboy novels of Zane Grey comprised some of her favourite reading choices.

Molly and her siblings went to school in a two-room schoolhouse, with the first five grades in one room, and the rest in the other. There were two teachers who divided the students between them. Molly was a lively child, full of mischief, and well liked, excelling in mathematics and geography, learning skills that would serve her well in her future career. She remembered her teacher with affection: "Annie Romel! I'll never forget. She was an old tarter but she loved my mother. I think she favoured us kids, Jean and I, and was nice to us. But, boy oh boy, you got by with nothing. You studied and you worked."

Summer was Molly's favourite time of year, when

From Raw Lumber to Ships' Masts

Rough-cut lumber was harvested in the interior and sent to, or processed in, lumber ports. From these ports, the rough-cut or processed lumber was shipped to markets all over North America. Some of these products were shingles, tan bark, masts, telephone poles, and railroad ties.

she could be with her father on the *Jean K* during the long weeks of vacation. An excellent teacher, Paul Kool instructed the young Molly and she soon learned everything she needed to know about navigation. As a teenager, Molly became a master at repairing the engine, running the winch, handling the lines, and setting the sails. She could sew canvas, splice rope, and cook. She learned how to steer through treacherous waters without electronic aid, but by compass, watch, tide, and time. "You really had to be able to read the weather pretty well. There was radio, but they weren't very good with the weather, any more than they are today," she chuckled. "We didn't have a barometer, so you learned to read all the signs. It got so my father depended more on me than he did on himself. He said I could smell the weather."

Since the early 1800s, scowing had been common along the Petitcodiac River from Alma to Moncton, helping to nurture commerce in the villages along its banks. In the meantime, Moncton was on its way to becoming the second largest city in New Brunswick. Its busy port was full of cargo ships from the United States and Europe, ready to load timber and other goods for outward journeys. While schooners and cargo ships had to remain farther offshore so they could stay afloat, scows could sail close to land at high tide, then rest on their flat bottoms as the tide went out, high and dry, while being loaded. These tough little boats hauled wood products and stone that was used as foundations during the building boom. They visited wharves on both sides of the Petitcodiac River, from Moncton to Hopewell Cape and crossed the challenging waters of the Bay of Fundy to Joggins, Shulie, Apple River, and Sand River.

Spring and summer in Moncton brought heavy rains, turning the city's streets into a quagmire. What better solution than gravel, hauled by the scows and deposited on the main streets of town? Scows could travel at a speed of about thirteen kilometres per hour up the river from Hopewell Cape to Moncton. Their arrival and departure times were always uncertain, depending as they did on arriving just before high tide. There were just a few hours to unload and still have enough water in the river to go back downstream to Hopewell Cape, where other scows waited for the tide to carry them back upriver. The scows stopped in the current by throwing out an anchor, and were then turned by the current to face downstream and moored to the wharf. The time of day had no bearing on the work; the scows travelled in darkness or daylight, as long as the tides were right. It was a full day's and often a full-night's work as men waited on the wharves at all hours, searching for a glimpse of running lights in gathering darkness, ready to take the mooring lines. If a scow took longer to unload after the high tide, the crew was resigned to wait twelve hours until the next high tide. At low tide, the scows rested on the flat, rocky bottom alongside the wharf. The scows hauled an average of two loads each week, more in good weather.

Captain Kool celebrates her achievement with friends. "They [other women] never went on and did anything about it. Not like I did."

CHAPTER THREE

A CHILD OF THE DEPRESSION

As she entered her mid-teens, Molly began to consider her job options. She briefly considered pursuing a nursing career when she graduated from high school, a common choice for women. The training cost money, however, and there was none in the Kool family to finance her. Descended from a long line of seafarers, Molly knew from an early age that she preferred to spend her life on the ocean.

She still had a few more school terms—and more summer vacations when she was free to spend time on the *Jean K* with her father, who would hire two men to replace her in the fall. During this time, she honed her skills as she sailed up the Saint John River with her father, around shifting sandbars to pick up lumber from the mill just below Fredericton or hauling gravel. Molly and her sister Jean sometimes sailed together, but Jean suffered from seasickness. She ultimately decided to stay home and look after their mother while Molly and her brother John worked on the *Jean K*, learning under their father's guidance.

Besides reading the weather and facing the daunting tides of the Bay of Fundy, Molly learned to navigate the Reversing Falls, a series of rapids on the Saint John River in Saint John, where the river runs through a narrow gorge before emptying into the Bay of Fundy. At this location, the waters coming out of the bay are forced to reverse by the incoming tide, creating an even higher wave that is dangerous for vessels about to exit or enter the river. As a result, vessels must wait for slack tide when conditions are calm, before they can enter. According to Molly, timing was everything.

> Well, if you go through a little too late it can be quite hairy. Or a little too early. I've been through them a lot of times. But you wait until half tide and it's okay. It's just as calm as here. But you get a little bit late or you take it a little bit early, then you're standing on the wheel, real hard. You had to watch where you were going for a few minutes there. Those whirlpools would move you around a little bit, coming down through the maelstrom there, the Old Sow, down Deer Island, Campobello, just across from Eastport. You've got that tremendous tide running through there, and the southwest wind coming up against you. That's a very treacherous spot.

Sleep was a rare commodity in rough weather and often Molly and her crew found themselves fighting for their lives and their ship. One particular spot on Black River that could only be approached at high tide was built like a funnel, with high sea surges. As Molly de-

The Reversing Falls Bridge in Saint John, NB.

scribes it, "there was a breakwater there. And we'd go in and try to go up that breakwater. But then the surge of the sea coming in would part your lines. So you'd be putting out new lines all the time. And then when the tide would go out, you'd splice them and get back for the next session."

With all this experience under her belt, Molly completed grade ten, and was ready to begin her career in earnest. At that time, a certain company name was becoming more and more prominent in the news. K. C. Irving Enterprises included an energy processing, transporting, and marketing company headquartered in Saint John. Today, Irving employs over seven thousand people, in seven hundred fueling locations, thirteen marine ter-

The Highest in the World

At low tide, the water in the Bay of Fundy is four metres lower than the natural level of the Saint John River. At that time, the flow of the river is downstream over the rapids into the Bay of Fundy. When the tide changes, the water level in the Bay of Fundy gradually rises until slack tide, which is three hours after low tide. That is the point when the water level of the Bay of Fundy is even with the natural level of the Saint John River. For twenty minutes the water is absolutely still with no rapids, and only at that time can boats safely navigate through the Reversing Falls. Over the next three hours, as the water level in the Bay of Fundy keeps rising to a level higher than that of the Saint John River, the water in the river flows upstream over the rapids. The force of the high tide pushes the river water so far upstream that it can be felt in Fredericton 120 kilometres away.

minals, and a delivery fleet of tractor-trailers. Irving was just a fledgling company in 1925, but its presence in the form of tankers in the Bay of Fundy caught Molly's attention.

"Oh yes, Irving was really starting to make his play," recalled Molly, remembering that K.C. had some small, recently acquired tankers in the bay. She knew Irving would need a licensed master to run them, and she thought about applying for a job on one of them. Paul Kool was not in good health, however, and this caused Molly to abandon the idea of leaving home to work for Irving. Although Molly never applied for a job there, and never met K. C., he soon came to know her when she made newspaper headlines.

Canada was especially hard hit by the Great Depression that followed the crash of the US stock market in October 1929. Unemployment soared with 30 percent of the labour force jobless, industrial production collapsed, and prices fell rapidly with the lowered demand for consumer goods. In 1933, one-fifth of the Canadian population became dependent on government assistance, but tens of thousands were too proud to fall back on charity. Jobless men drifted from the east to the west, riding the rods or starving in city alleyways. Eviction notices for non-payment of rent were common and Molly recalled seeing beggars in Saint John, asking for handouts and living miserable lives by the waterfront.

Men and women alike resented wage-earning women for taking away income from family men, and petitions sprang up to bar women from working unless it was absolutely necessary for their survival. Those women who held onto their jobs received drastic wage cuts. A government-issued poster asked in blazing text, "Do you feel justified in holding a job which could be filled by a man who has not only himself to support, but a wife and family as well?"[5]

"I'm a child of the Depression," Molly once said, pointing out that the family home had neither electricity nor running water. Helping to bring in the family income was vital and as soon as she finished school, Molly went straight to work. "Well, I came out of school during the Great Depression. My father had a small vessel. He needed a seaman and I needed a job. So I started going to sea."

She had been accustomed to summer work with her father, but winters were a different experience. "It was

"Sometimes when we were in a rough spot, Dad would get up and take the wheel. I always felt I had him to confide in."

pure hell. You fought the cold, you fought the storms, you fought the ice, you would have to get into these small ports and get back out before it froze over again."

Molly and the crew were always at the mercy of the tides, which could be both friend and foe. "When you went out, you were out with no harbour for at least six hours. It wasn't an easy life, but it was the only life I knew. You'd catch a couple hours sleep, then get up and get on your way and hope you hadn't judged the weather wrong. But if you were going to make a living, you had to take some chances."

Paul Kool taught Molly at an early age how to use
the barometer, then took her advice without question,
almost believing that Molly knew better than he.

Molly's father had taught her at an early age how
to use a barometer, and Molly had since developed
such skill in correctly predicting weather that her father deferred to her whenever there was doubt about
weather trends. He took her advice without question,
almost believing that Molly knew better than he. Molly

admired her father for his ability to recognize the horizon during any kind of weather, and the way he could anchor without having to run a lead line to get the depth. On the Bay of Fundy, he could tell where the land was and his distance from it without instruments, something that did not yet come instinctively to Molly. She depended on her father to take the wheel whenever she was in doubt.

Molly attracted a fair number of suitors, even though working on board a vessel did not allow a young woman to look or feel feminine in any way, especially in winter weather. In the summertime, a pair of slacks and a shirt sufficed, but working in cold winter winds meant wearing thick layers of woollen underwear, heavy sweaters, and a leather jacket. Hip waders were useful for crossing from boat to shore. It was a matter of piling on as many clothes as could keep her warm without impeding her activities on board. Molly's mother made her double-knit mitts, but heaving the lead line to find out the water depth soaked them and transformed them into an uncomfortable, soggy mass.

In spite of all this, Molly and her crew might go to dances at the Seaman's Club in their time off, usually while waiting for the tide to change. She met her first love during her initial year of full-time work. The *Jean K* was one of those many small vessels that carried freight from the shore out to the bigger ships lying at anchor in deep water, plying larger waters from Saint John to

The *Jean K* ties up at a wharf. "You'd catch a couple of hours sleep, then get up and get on your way."

The Maritime Scow, Tried and True

The Maritime scow was a craft with a very distinctive hull design. The scow had a flat bottom and flat sides, giving it a boxy appearance. Scows were useful for carrying goods to ports, piers, and beaches, and for sailing in rivers and bays. They were used from the early 1800s through the early 1900s and were a valuable means of transport because they could carry a heavy load yet their keels sat not far below the waterline. They were inexpensive to build and operate. Scows were most often rigged as sloops or schooners.

By the late nineteenth century, the sailing scow was no longer in use. Its boxy hull shape was adopted in the building of the later unrigged steel barges that are used today.

The *Jean K* rests on the river bottom at low tide.

Boston. The *Jean K* also sailed up little creeks to deliver goods. One such contract was to haul gravel to the building site of the first CBC international short-wave radio station on the marsh between Sackville and Aulac. The *Jean K* went up a creek in the Tantramar Marshes and landed in a farmer's backyard at his dock. During this work, Molly met a farm labourer named Curtis. "I don't think it got serious, I was only eighteen," said Molly. "Finally, the job was finished and we were gone. Curtis came to Alma a couple of times to see me. Guess we must have wrote letters and I said when I would be home for Christmas that year. I knit him a sweater." Curtis didn't acknowledge the gift. "Guess he didn't like the sweater. I never heard from him again. By this time there was another port and someone else."

The idea of working toward a master's certificate was foremost in Molly's mind. Before then, mariners on small vessels like the *Jean K* did not need to have a license, but by the time Molly had worked for two years full-time on the vessel, a new law was passed that required mariners of small vessels to be licensed. Seasoned sailors could apply to qualify, based only on their time and experience, but Molly needed more schooling and time at sea. She saw an opportunity to earn a license for herself and was undeterred by the fact that she was entering a man's domain. She knew some of the history of women at sea, who sailed with their captain husbands in the old sailing vessels. She also knew that no woman had ever earned a license, although she imagined many of them were better sailors than she. "They never went on and did anything about it—not like I did," said Molly. She was probably referring to women like Bessie Pritchard Hall, who went to sea with her captain father and took command when the crew fell ill, sailing across the Atlantic.

The *Jean K* carried lumber to Saint John in the winter, and was often docked there for weeks until the weather and tides were right. Molly used this time to attend navigation school in the Old Customs Building on Prince William Street. Most of the other students, all men, were studying navigation before learning how to fly in the armed forces.

"I felt that if I could get a license, I could earn a better living and I wouldn't have to depend on washing dishes or making beds. I guess I was ambitious, and wanted to make a better life for myself. I think that I was very well loved, and especially by the guys that were captains of these rigs." The seafaring men in Molly's circle enthusiastically supported her ambition. "I can remember old Captain Lawson saying when I was going for my license—he was one of the old schooner men that carried you across the Atlantic—and he said, 'Molly, you're going for your deep-water license.' I said, 'I can't, I don't have any deep-water time.' He said, 'My God, come with me, Molly. We'll put her out in deep water, and we'll keep her there.' Most of them were just so pleased that I was trying to do something that their sons weren't trying to do."

Molly was fully aware that the language of the new law was gender specific. "They did make a provision that allowed these men—and I say men—an opportunity to take an oral exam and they could get a service certificate. Well, I saw an opportunity there." Molly was not deterred by the fact that she couldn't obtain the service certificate unless she was actually the captain of the vessel. She had a plan to work around that. She knew she could get a certificate if she went the long route and earned a mate's license first, and then worked for the master's.

Molly and fourteen boys enrolled to study for the mate's license. Their instructor, Captain Richard Pollock, struck by Molly's eagerness to learn and the novelty of having a female student for the first time in his life, helped her as much as he could. He would pace the room looking at his students' work, occasionally patting Molly on the shoulder in encouragement, saying "Molly, my only girl." Molly took it all in stride, learning quickly, and matching the boys' output. The lessons continued through the winter and into spring and after four months of intensive study, it was time for spring exams. Since there was no examiner in Saint John, one was called for in Yarmouth. Molly was pleased to note that she was treated the same as everybody else during the exam. She passed with distinction, even though some of the boys did not pass at all. Now she could sign on with the *Jean K* as mate.

She received some media attention when she earned her mate's license, but it was a small flutter compared to what would come later. Captain Pollock proclaimed that Molly was one of his best students ever, and he and Molly were photographed together for the newspaper stories. Not long after this event she had a run-in with a Norwegian steamer that brought her even more publicity.

Molly, her father, and the crew had come upriver to Moncton with a load of lumber and tied up at the wharf alongside another scow to wait for the next day's high tide. Around a bend in the river steamed the *Salamis*, a Norwegian vessel from Barbados with a cargo of molasses. Captain Gunderson hailed the two scows, asking them to move so their vessel could tie up. The other scow obediently moved away and tied up to a smaller wharf

First Woman Captain of an Ocean-going Vessel

Anna Ivanovna Shchetinina (1908–1999) was a Soviet merchant marine sailor, said to be the world's first woman captain of an ocean-going vessel, predating Molly Kool by several years. Shchetinina was born near Vladivostok into a family of a railway switchmen. She graduated from the Vladivostok Marine School then worked with a shipping company where she started as an ordinary seaman. She rose through the ranks from second mate to captain at the age of twenty-seven, the first woman to command an ocean-going ship. She garnered world attention in 1935 when she made her first voyage on the MV *Chavycha* from Hamburg, around Europe, Africa and Asia. She served in the Baltic during World War Two, receiving a medal for her courage at sea. In 1951, she became a senior instructor at the Leningrad Marine Engineering College, and later the dean of the college's Navigation Department. A monument to honour her name stands in Vladivostock.

along the river, but Molly refused to budge. It was imperative to move the *Jean K* out of the way; otherwise, the captain of the *Salamis* was in danger of being stuck at low tide and losing his ship and its cargo.

"Where's the harbourmaster?" demanded Captain Gunderson.

"What do you want the harbourmaster for?" asked Molly.

Hearing a woman's voice, Captain Gunderson thought his battle was easily won, but he didn't know he was up against the redoubtable Molly Kool.

"You're talking to Mate Molly Kool. I was here first and I'm staying," stated Molly. The steamer moved closer until it was up against the *Jean K*. Two seamen boarded Molly's scow intending to cast off her mooring lines, but Molly was there to meet them with a piece of lumber in hand. The seamen got off her deck in short order. Epithets flew through the air, including "petticoat skipper." Molly made it clear she was not going to be bossed around by a Norwegian. Gunderson, in cold fury, aimed his freighter at the *Jean K* and moved ahead, nudging the scow two or three times until her mooring lines parted and she drifted downstream.

Gunderson took the coveted place at the wharf, then reverted to gentleman and called into the darkness, "Do you want me to throw you a line?"

"You've been throwing me a line for the past hour," retorted Molly. "You cut me adrift. I know my marine laws. I'll see you in marine court." [6]

The *Jean K* was grounded on the riverbank but refloated at the next tide. The case was settled out of court in Molly's favour, and Molly again made the headlines for proving herself as good as any man.

For the next two years, it was business as usual for Molly, but she was bent on working toward her master's license and serving the requisite time on the boat. The next two years went quickly and the time came to put in her application at the Marine Institute in Yarmouth for the master's license. Her application was refused pointblank. No woman had ever applied in the Institute's history, and there was no hope that they would allow it now. Undaunted, Molly applied again. She was again

Until Paul Kool built a wheelhouse on the *Jean K*, navigating during the winters was cold, hard work. "You were outdoors to the elements all the time."

refused. When she pressed her case, it was carefully explained to her that no feminine pronouns were used in the Canada Shipping Act, and no provisions were made in case a woman ever acquired the experience and ability to command a vessel. This was offered as proof that a woman should certainly not apply for an examination to obtain a master's license. A clause in the Canada Shipping Act at that time reflects the gender bias that Molly was up against:

> The Board of Trade shall deliver to every applicant who is duly reported by the examiners to have passed the examination satisfactorily, and to have given satisfactory evidence of his sobriety, his experience, his ability, and his general good conduct on board ship, such a certificate of competency as the case requires.

Molly persisted, but before she could sit for the exam, the wording of the Act needed to be changed. "There was no 'she' in the Canada Shipping Act," remembered Molly, "so they tell me they did change it. I didn't know that, but they tell me they did."

Perhaps it was the increasing media attention, combined with more modern ideas about the rights of women in society that helped her case. Whatever the influence, the Act was changed. Molly was allowed to register and began making waves.

This time, her testing differed from the men's. Molly knew it was because of her gender that she was subjected to some extra scrutiny. She soon learned that it wasn't enough that the regular examiner oversee her test; instead, a chief examiner from Halifax had to be called for. Molly waited two more weeks before they sent him from Halifax. His name was Captain Waterhouse, and he was to assist the local examiner, Captain Hilton. Molly was required to sit alone. There were boys ready to be examined, but they were not allowed to sit the exam while Molly was in the room—they might be too distracted and this would spoil their results. When Molly went to the examiner's office, a telegram awaited her from her father giving her the boost in confidence that she needed. It read, "Go ahead, Molly. I know you can do it!"

She was very nervous, aware that she was setting a precedent and worried that the examiners might ask trick questions to try and fail her. Her answers had to be 100 percent correct in both the oral and written exam or she would certainly fail. She took her oral and written examinations over two anxious days. She was tested on subjects that covered first aid, chart work, and navigation safety.

"Captain Waterhouse talked to me and somehow, someway, I convinced him I was a seaman," she said. She passed and became Canada's first woman master mariner. Her new status entitled her to command a steam- or motor-propelled vessel anywhere on the coast of North America.

Molly cabled home with these famous words: "Call me Captain from now on!"

Now Molly was entitled to wear the peaked cap and greatcoat with brass buttons that reflected her rank. Local media took note of her achievement, and the news soon spread along the entire East Coast. It seemed that from then on, anything Molly Kool did was news. Molly modestly took no credit for the fact that the Canadian shipping law was changed to accommodate her, but the wording in the Canada Shipping Act became distinctly gender-neutral because of Captain Molly Kool. A "certificated person" means a person who holds a Master or Mate certificate valid for the vessel on which the craft is carried. [6]

Thanks to the Persons Case of 1929, there was no longer any question that this definition included Molly Kool.

Molly's achievement brought media attention on both sides of the border.
Here, a reporter poses with Molly.

CHAPTER FOUR
BELIEVE IT!

WITH A MASTER'S ticket in her pocket, Molly was ready to make a start at her hard-won career. Back in Saint John the next day, she signed on as captain of the *Jean K*. Her father was often too ill to sail with her, and she felt the loss of her mentor despite her own credentials as a skipper. Her brother John never studied for a master's certificate, but he called himself captain whenever he took over from Molly. As captain, Molly usually worked twelve-hour days, and all on board were responsible for the difficult tasks of heaving the anchor or pumping the bilge. Everybody pitched in. "I'm sure that none of them would do it today," said Molly. "Things are more automated now!"

Saint John, a strategic location as the largest port on the East Coast, was the usual base for the *Jean K*. Molly and the crew kept busy in the winter, hauling lumber and pulp from ports such as Big Salmon River, Saint Martins, Little Salmon River, Point Wolfe, and Alma. They were paid by the board foot. They continued to haul weir material from St. Stephen to Grand Manan Island. Molly would collect materials from Seaboard Paper and

MacKay Lumber in Saint John and gravel from Sherman Blakeny in Moncton. Up and down the coast, the *Jean K* plied the waters, going wherever work needed to be done.

Paul Kool was relieved to have Molly take command. When he was able to sail with her, he gave advice when it was asked for. He sometimes took over when Molly was unsure about steering through rough patches, although her years of experience had stood her in good stead. Sailing on one of the roughest seas in the world meant they had to be alert for storms brewing. Getting back into port might be easy when the tide was in, but if it was out, they had to sail through it as best they could. Fog was always a challenge and Molly developed an instinct for finding her way through dangerous fog conditions and threatening riptides that no classroom instruction could have taught. Still, she had always worked at her father's side, and as she took the wheel, she felt comfort from his presence when he was on board.

Molly knew her physical limitations. "One thing I didn't do was stow lumber. That was a little bit too much for me. I tried it one day but I just wasn't up to that."

If stowing the lumber on deck was too much for the petite Molly, shifting tons of gravel was a job she performed alongside everyone else, shoveling it into wheelbarrows and wheeling it along catwalks onto the deck. It would take two tides, or twelve hours, to load such an amount, because it could only be done at low tide when they could lie close to a sandbar.

"And because this crew didn't run the ship, you had to have your cargo and do everything of that nature as well," she recalled, "and you usually took two tides to load. But then after I'd been going with Dad a short time, he rigged up a little donkey engine that we could use as a scoop and one man could do the work of two. So, sometimes we could load between tides. And that would shorten up our turnaround time so that we could make a little bit more money. But it was actually back-breaking labour."

There was danger everywhere. Molly's vessel caught fire when the gas tank of the *Jean K* exploded as they were hauling pulp from Swan's Island. The aft end of the vessel burned to the water's edge, almost destroying the entire boat. Insurance was expensive and not many could afford the high rates, the Kool family included. Repairs from any accidents that happened to the *Jean K* came out of the Kool family's pocket. But Molly's brother reconstructed the boat and they were back in business.

When the *Jean K* was hauling scrap iron, it affected the magnetic compass. On one occasion, the scow was running up the bay towards Grand Manan Island, and Molly was on the lookout for some rock ledges named "the Wolves." Because of the load, the compass bearings were slightly off and the ledges suddenly appeared directly ahead. "But we didn't hit," remembered Molly. "I hauled hard for it and we scraped by them. But there was all sorts of things like this that happened. I mean it was in a day's work."

During an unloading of lumber in Saint John, Molly was standing on the icy dock when she slipped and fell four and a half metres to the deck below. She crawled into her bunk and by the next morning, realized her leg was broken. The crew called a doctor who sent her to the nearest hospital, but Molly did not want to take time off. "You have to do something so I could at least get into the wheelhouse," said Molly. Her crew insisted that she take time off work, and broke down her resistance until she eventually gave in. She was housebound for eight weeks. Molly had taken the occasional break when the crew was forced into port by bad weather and they would often spend a few hours at the Seaman's Club in Saint John, waiting it out. But she had never taken this much time away from work. The interminable wait was a personal hell for Molly, but the *Jean K* tied up in Alma for the winter in spite of her protests to allow her leg to heal.

By the spring, Molly was back on board. On one trip to load lumber in Point Wolfe with her father and crew, they were just returning to Saint John in fog when they heard a boat horn and knew a ship was bearing down on them. It was a passenger vessel, the SS *Yarmouth*. As the scow tried to steer clear, the bow of the *Yarmouth* caught the deck load of lumber on the scow. The lumber was stacked in the usual way, with the second tier protruding a metre or so over the first, and it was this load that saved their hull from the impact. Molly had been at the wheel and her father on lookout. With foresight, the crew jumped onto the deck load of lumber when they knew a collision was coming. Her father shouted for Molly to jump up with them, but before she could, the jarring force knocked her over the side. She plunged under the scow, narrowly missing the suction of the propellers, and came up on the other side. "I could have been chopped to little bits, but it happened so fast. I was up on the other side, and there was part of the deck load

Accidents on deck were common in icy weather. Molly and a friend show off their broken limbs.

floating around, so I just grabbed it. Of course, I was a good swimmer, but the cold! Cripes, it makes me cold just to think about it. It happened so fast that you didn't

Romance, Rhythm, and Ripley

Robert Ripley creator of *Ripley's Believe it or Not*®, brought his program to radio in April 1930. His debut was a hit, and he began a weekly broadcast on NBC, By 1944, he could be heard five nights every week. Highlights of his programs were *Romance, Rhythm, and Ripley*, CBS, in 1945, and *Pages from Robert L. Ripley's Radio Scrapbook* in 1947–48.

Robert Ripley was the first to attempt many of his endeavours, broadcasting nationwide on a radio network from mid-ocean, then from Buenos Aires to New York, and eventually, with the help of translators, to every nation in the world simultaneously.

even know it happened." Molly joked that she was in more danger trying to duck the detritus that was thrown to her by the crew on deck.

With this experience and others it was natural that Molly was very cautious in the fog. On another trip not long after the collision, something black loomed up ahead in the mist, and Molly yelled, "Hard to port!" not wanting a repeat adventure. It was a whale, much to Molly's relief.

Molly often captained the scow without Paul Kool on board and one afternoon, after hauling veneer logs, she made her way back to port in Saint John to pick up her father. When she arrived at the wharf in Saint John, a boat was already alongside. Molly came in too close, and the overhanging bridge on this boat took the rigging off her scow. Molly, like an errant teenager who had crashed the family car, guessed her father would be furi-

"She's twenty-four, has long blonde hair and pretty blue eyes. In fact, she looks like any debutante you might find on Fifth Avenue," said Robert Ripley.

ous. She went looking for him in town to break the news. "Dad, I just took the mast out of her," she told him, expecting anger, but Paul Kool, with his mild disposition, took it in stride. "Well, anyone could do that," he said.

A female sea captain in that era was a marvel, so is it any wonder that Molly was contacted to go on Robert Ripley's radio show? The iconic show, *Ripley's Believe It or Not®*, dealt in bizarre events and items so strange and unusual that listeners might question its claims. Beginning in 1918, Robert Ripley made a career out of hunting for the bizarre in everyday life, including a

June 6, 1940

Miss Mollie Kool
Alma, New Brunswick
Canada

Dear Miss Kool:

Mr. Ripley has learned of how
you became captain of a cargo vessel at
the age of 23.

If a suitable spot could be
arranged, would you be willing to come to
New York as Mr. Ripley's guest and appear on a Believe It or Not program? We
enclose a form for our files which we
would like you to fill out and return to
us at your convenience.

May we hear from you?

BELIEVE IT OR NOT

Don McClure

M

An invitation to appear on Ripley's show. "I was
thrilled to go to New York," said Molly.

car hurdler, a painting on a canvas of human flesh, or
an unopened deck of cards in a narrow-necked bottle.
The letter of invitation to Molly from Ripley arrived
on June 6, 1940, but of course, Captain Kool was not
at home to receive it. In fact, she was unable to receive
any mail, as she was at sea somewhere near Montreal.
Her sister Jean responded to Mr. Ripley's letter and sent
along Molly's two scrapbooks full of press clippings
from Canadian, British, and American newspapers. A
few days later, Molly mailed her letter of acceptance,

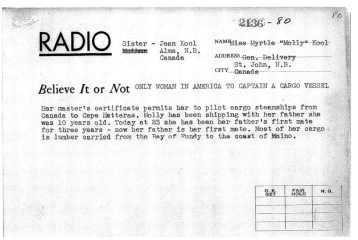

RADIO

Sister - Jean Kool
Mother Alma, N.B.
Canada

NAME Miss Myrtle "Molly" Kool
ADDRESS Gen. Delivery
St. John, N.B.
CITY Canada

Believe It or Not ONLY WOMAN IN AMERICA TO CAPTAIN A CARGO VESSEL

Her master's certificate permits her to pilot cargo steamships from
Canada to Cape Hatteras. Molly has been shipping with her father she
was 10 years old. Today at 23 she has been her father's first mate
for three years - now her father is her first mate. Most of her cargo
is lumber carried from the Bay of Fundy to the coast of Maine.

O.K. GET	FAIR HOLD	N. G.

Jean Kool's reply for Molly, who was somewhere at sea.

and in late October, she was en route to New York City.

"I was thrilled to go to New York, all expenses paid, and I received pay for it," remembered Molly. Ripley arranged the train fare from Saint John to New York, but Molly requested a bus ticket instead. The agent booked a hotel room at the Taft for her and sent her an extra ten dollars to handle the tips and meals. It was suggested that perhaps she might like to see a movie in her free time. Molly travelled from Saint John to Boston and from there to Grand Central Station in New York. She had visited New York previously and was familiar with the bustling city, but she asked to be met at the station. "Very important," she emphasized in her cable.

Robert Ripley presented Molly as a "Ripley's Believe It or Not® of the Sea." Along with her were two other women: Josie Bishop, an elderly woman who owned her own radium mine, and Helen Bullock, billed as a "wom-

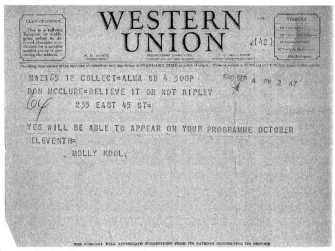

© 2011 Ripley Entertainment Inc

Captain Kool confirms her appearance on Ripley's show.

an woodchopper." It is likely that the radio audience was duly impressed by the spirited Molly Kool and the stories she told. Television had not yet been invented, so to begin with, a description of Molly was in order. "She's twenty-four years old, has long blonde hair, and pretty blue eyes. In fact, she looks like any young debutante you might see on Fifth Avenue," stated Ripley.

Asked to describe her boat, Molly sounded almost clipped in her description of the *Jean K*: "Length—a hundred feet; seven-foot draft and a twenty-two-foot beam displacement—132 tons, powered by two diesel motors; and makes about seven knots. I have a crew of nine—all men." Molly told them that becoming a sea captain was something that ran in the family and attested to doing the hard work of any sailor, from scrubbing the decks to climbing the rigging. Ripley asked her if she did all the work of a sailor, and she replied in the affirmative. "No one did me any favours," she said, and gave a word of warning to women who might want to follow in her footsteps: "A woman sea captain doesn't get many calls. The shipowners' wives won't let their husbands hire a woman captain." Ripley asked how a woman like Molly, feminine in every way, could be a sea captain. Weren't sea captains always "old and rough and dirty, like Barnacle Bill?" Ripley was probably referring to the famous verse from the traditional drinking song "Barnacle Bill the Sailor":

I'll sail the sea until I croak,
Drink my whiskey, swear, and smoke,
But I can't swim a bloody stroke,
Said Barnacle Bill the Sailor.[6]

Molly stated that she could take care of herself. She described the set-to with the Norwegian captain who called her a "petticoat skipper" and ordered her to get her boat out of the way. When she refused and the captain sent a sailor to deal with her, "I grabbed a belaying pin from the rail and told him to get off my ship. As soon as he saw the belaying pin, he beat it." She continued with her story: "The captain sent a bigger fellow. As soon as he walked on deck, I walked behind him, swung him around, and hit him a sweet right to the chin. Then I put the boot to him and he went over the side of the ship and I said, 'Captain, if you want the lines cast off, come down and try it yourself.' He didn't!" She stated that she was ready to go to war. After all, as a captain in the Canadian merchant navy, it was her duty and she was ready for it. [7]

Molly demonstrates her knock-out punch. "I walked behind him, swung him around and hit him a sweet right to the chin."

Molly's appearance on Ripley's radio show revealed how easily she could switch from one lifestyle to another. A few weeks after she returned from New York, she was plunged into a challenge that was to prove one of the greatest tests of her luck and skills as a navigator. It happened just before Christmas, during a fierce winter storm off Cape Spencer, east of Saint John.

The *Jean K* was rounding Cape Spencer in a heavy wind. Molly was at the wheel and her father on lookout when one of the engines failed and the sail ripped apart in the winds. Without engine power, the scow drifted through smashing waves toward the rocks until it began to sink. The crew was left standing knee-deep in the raging sea. Molly described it this way:

> We were running down the bay in a sou'easter, which is bad in the Bay of Fundy, and you've got a riptide there anyway to begin with, so it's very rough. We began taking on water, and we finally lost one engine. All you could see were the rocks, with the waves smashing against them, and I knew we were looking at sure death. We put the sail on, but we lost part of that, so we only had about a half a sail. Then we lost the wheel ropes, so that we had nothing to steer with, and this is why I say that my father is a good sailor. He got those wheel ropes repaired.

The wind suddenly shifted westward, and the scow staggered to shelter.

> We worked her into a little cove just beyond the cape. By this time, we're full of water, so we anchored. The light keeper and his son had come down to this beach area there, so we got in the boat and we went ashore. They met us right there as the surf's rolling in, so we're on top of the surf—and they grabbed the boat and pulled us up high and dry on the beach, and took us up to the lighthouse. Now that was poverty, if I ever saw it. I think there were two small children in there—it was clean,

immaculate, white floors, all scrubbed—with just diapers on, wood stove. He had a horse and sleigh I guess, and he took us to the nearest telephone, where we could call someone to come and get us. The next day, the wind had died down, and we got the tugboat and went out and picked her up, took her in and drained her out and got her ready to go back to sea again. We lost the deck load of course.

Molly and the crew were safely home for Christmas.

Along with the moments of dire challenge, there were many more long hours of waiting for the weather to break or the tide to come in. Card games like crib helped to fill them. The crew would keep the little wood-burning oven lit, often frying fish, usually harbour pollock, on the cooktop, and there was always a pot of coffee warming. There was no refrigeration, and being out for long hours meant a diet of canned meat with the occasional fish or lobster for variety. "I never did like canned milk. But it didn't bother anybody else. They'd even eat it on cereal, but that wasn't for me." Molly would fish from the deck for harbour pollock and fry them up, or if they were scarce, she would fry corned beef or make a stew.

Although her father was in poor health and suffered from ulcers, he sailed with Molly as much as he could, lying in one of the bunks when he felt unwell. "When we first had the boat, we didn't have a wheelhouse. That was bad especially in the winter because you were outdoors to the elements all the time. But then we built the wheelhouse on." Paul Kool was there to offer advice when Molly asked for it, his calm demeanour a boost whenever her confidence wavered. "I'd be talking with

The "Sparks" of World War Two

Of those women who served during World War Two, only a few are known. Many were lost in the line of duty, and no histories survive them. Fern Blodget, born in 1918, grew up in Cobourg, Ontario, at the same time that Molly Kool was sailing with her father on the *Jean K.* Fern had always dreamed of becoming a sailor. When war broke out in 1939, the merchant marine began recruiting wireless operators in Canada. She applied three times before being taken seriously, attended night school while work-ing at a full-time job during the day, and passed her exams at the top of her class. A call to go to sea arrived on graduation day.

Fern had often told her radio-school principal that she would like to become a ship's radio operator, or "sparks," and with his help, she landed her first job on a Norwegian ship berthed in Montreal. When she arrived, her employers were disappointed that F. Blodgett was a woman. The captain was badly in need of a sparks, and could not wait a day longer. Fern was hired. Once out of the St. Lawrence River, Fern became violently seasick. With a bucket at her feet, she carried on, and soon found her sea legs.

She went on to become chief operator of the *Mosedale* and made seventy-eight crossings. She witnessed many deaths at sea, and when asked why she did this work, she replied, "Why should I not risk my life when millions of men are risking theirs? Is a woman's life more precious than a man's?" Fern lived in Norway after the war and was awarded a medal in 1988 in recognition of the special distinction she had brought to her city. She had earlier received a medal from the Norwegian government for her wartime services.

him and getting his advice on things, because he was right there with me. And sometimes, especially in the first few years that I was there and we'd get in a rough channel or have some problems, Dad would get up and take the wheel. And I always felt that I had him to con-fide in and talk to."

Women in the Navy

Although women played only a small role in the Canadian merchant navy, some pioneers worked as stewardesses, and a few Canadian women were radio officers on ships of the Norwegian merchant navy. (This was the only Allied merchant fleet that permitted women to serve aboard ships as wireless operators at that time.) Since many of these women had their lives cut short before they could establish families of their own, and because women's efforts were not given the same recognition as men's, very little is known about them. In some instances, their names, ships, and length of service at sea are available in the records.

Molly, acting as her own broker, made deals with the big lumber companies to haul lumber and gravel up the Petitcodiac River to Saint John. More than once she fell overboard during times of choppy seas and high winds, but she kept going anyway. It was all routine for Molly. She did her work without electronic devices or any modern-day navigation equipment. Like other captains of that era, Molly relied on lighthouses and marker buoys; she knew where they were supposed to be, and hoped she'd find them in the fog.

By this time, Canada was at war and there were many foreign ships and officers in port. The stimulus of wartime demand ended the Depression in the Maritimes and the rest of Canada. Industries revived and prices improved. Naval bases appeared along the Maritime coast, including Sydney in Nova Scotia, where a major naval base of world importance was established. Gunnery and anti-submarine warfare were practised in training facilities. Destroyers dotted the waters of quiet harbours to protect the coast from German submarines that ranged the waters from Newfoundland and on toward Florida and the Caribbean. Young men, formerly unemployed during the Depression, now seized the opportunity to train for the merchant navy or to earn commissioned ranks. Canadian ships carried troops and ammunition across the ocean to the fighting fronts. Until 1939, Canada had a dozen shipyards and only about five thousand shipbuilders. Now, there were one hundred thousand workers building everything from dories to destroyers.

On the home front, the Women's Institute organized fundraisers and knitting events, packed essentials such as jams and maple sugar, and sent goods off to the troops on the front. During the war years, only a small number of women served at sea. Canadian women who wanted to serve were faced with closed doors both during and after the war, as they were banned from serving on Canadian or Commonwealth ships. An official responded to a reporter's question about this issue in a horrified tone: "We have enough trouble on ships without having women on board!"[8]

Women were also forbidden to serve on foreign ships in Canadian ports, and were compelled to travel across the border to find work. Some Canadian women worked on Norwegian ships as radio operators because this merchant fleet was the only one that allowed women to serve. Since so many women who served lost their lives before they could have husbands and families of their own, very little is known about them.

Maude Elizabeth Steane, Ship's Radio Officer

Maude Elizabeth Steane, a ship's radio operator, had to leave Canada to find work, because women were not allowed to join any ship, Canadian or foreign, in Canada. Steane completed her wireless operator training at the Radio College of Canada in 1944, then joined the merchant ship SS *Viggo Hansteen* at New York. Just ten weeks after leaving home, Maude Steane was killed. One story says that she may have died by enemy gunfire. Other sources state that she was killed by a member of the SS *Viggo Hansteen's* crew. She was buried in the Allied War Cemetery near Florence, Italy.

During the start of the war, Molly was ready to serve in whatever capacity was required of her. Her preference was to work in the patrol boats in Halifax Harbour, but her father's lingering illness kept her close to home.

Most of the men Molly met were seamen who regarded her almost as a daughter and were proud of her. However, Molly did catch at least one young man's fancy. A Greek officer made a point of always being in port in Saint John just when Molly's boat arrived, so he could chat with the crew and get to know her. His ship was in dry dock for repairs for much of the winter. Molly and he began to see each other whenever she was in port, going to dances and other social events. One day he came on board the *Jean K* when Molly wasn't there. He planned to propose to Molly, but first asked her father for her hand in marriage. "Well, my father wasn't about to lose his fair-haired girl," said Molly, describing her father as one who tended to easily find fault with these would-be suitors. Paul Kool responded to the young man's approach with a roar of laughter, saying to the humbled officer, "I always thought you was a jackass, but that's the first time I ever really knew it."

When the war had just begun, the *Jean K* picked up a young seaman, a Norwegian, in Saint John as part of their crew. Molly and the crew sat on the deck eating lobsters and offered one to the seaman who, mystifyingly, did not know how to open the shellfish. Molly's brother told him to break off the claw first. The seaman did so, but immediately threw the claw in the water to the disbelief of the crew. He eventually signed off as a crew member, but a few days later, the RCMP visited Molly's boat with an interesting story. The crewman, whom the crew had believed to be Norwegian, was in fact a German spy, and had stolen her brother's papers.

Submarine warfare had broken out along the Atlantic seaboard during the winter of 1941 to 1942 with enemy submarines invading inland home waters and sinking merchant ships in the St. Lawrence River and the Gulf. Molly reported having seen the periscope of a U-boat rising out of the waters of the Bay of Fundy but no one quite believed her.

Molly was never sympathetic to the women's liberation movement, thinking it had gone too far with its talk of drafting women and putting them on the front lines. She didn't think the average woman was as strong as a man, but she didn't accept this easily: "I'll tell you, men today couldn't do what those men did. I wasn't able to do everything that they did because I wasn't strong enough, and that really pissed me off."

CHAPTER FIVE

SEA CHANGE

MOLLY FOUGHT the elements of wind and fog, always aware that not only the deck load, but also the lives of the crew, could be lost:

> There was bad luck and good luck, but this is in any phase of life, no matter what you do. You had to be fairly sure of yourself. You had to have the knowledge. And the working knowledge isn't something that you can learn in school. You have things you look for when it's foggy and you don't know where you're at. Like across from a headland you have a tide rip. And you know it's there and it's something that you only learn with experience. So you begin looking for these things. But you wouldn't learn that from a book. You'd have to have the practical knowledge to do it. You learn to respect the sea.

It was 1944 when Molly's life changed. She and her crew had been hauling material to build fish weirs from St. Stephen to Grand Manan, and were on their way to haul pulpwood from some of the islands in the bay to Bucksport. A woodlands manager came on board to meet Molly and take her up to the mill. They were taking a

Opposite page: Molly was Captain Richard Pollock's prize student. "Molly, my only girl," he would say.

New Brunswick's Leading Industry

In New Brunswick, timber was the major export and stimulated the growth of the province's other leading industries: shipbuilding, shipping, and agriculture. The timber trade required ships to carry wood to Britain, and in an era of wooden ships, New Brunswick had the material needed to construct them. Local investors , including the Cunard family, profited by lumbering in the Miramichi River basin. The Cunard family business became world-famous for its fleet of ocean-going ships.

The farmers in New Brunswick also benefitted from lumbering. While outgoing ships carried wood, incoming ones brought immigrants to work the land. These settlers sold timber from their farm lots (and from nearby Crown forests in which they trespassed), gaining a much-needed cash crop. In wintertime, farmers and their sons found jobs working at pulp-and-paper mills.

shortcut up the track along a trail littered with pieces of lumber, when a long splinter pierced Molly's foot. Molly was taken to the nursing station and a doctor called. Molly needed surgery to extract the splinter. She stayed at the Old Jed Prouty Inn for a week to recover, so that the doctor could continue to monitor her foot.

It was at the inn that Molly met Ray Blaisdell, a mill worker, and the man she was to marry. Not long after, Paul Kool became very ill and died in Alma. With this loss, Molly knew it was up to her to figure out where the riptides might be in deep fog, and she felt suddenly fearful about her abilities. Before this time, she had her father to talk to and consult, but now she had only herself.

A dream helped her to come to terms with her loss. One night she dreamt that the *Jean K* was in a very bad channel with whirlpools and rocks. Her father was with her, in the wheelhouse, and she asked him the question she was used to asking when things looked rough. "Dad, do you want to take the wheel?" In her dream, her father answered, "No, Molly. Go ahead. You can do it, girl." From then on, whenever Molly was in a tough spot, she remembered her father's words—"You can do it."

It was 1945 and the war had ended. Molly's courtship with Ray Blaisdell blossomed, and suddenly the comforts of a real home on dry land became more attractive to this tough woman who was used to a narrow bunk in the hold. "I didn't intend to stop, but I learned what it was like to go to bed every night in a warm bed. You didn't have to get up to see if you were dragging anchor, or if you had to get out with that tide—that tide!" she grimaced. "You know it wasn't the same as if you got up in the morning and went to a regular job." Molly turned down requests to take command of boats during these years. Her sister Jean sent her a clipping that advertised for a mate on one of the ferries running to Newfoundland, scarcely a challenge for Molly, but she decided she no longer wanted any part of sailing on the North Atlantic. "They would never have dared turn me down, but I was happy sitting at home."

Molly had been earning about three thousand dollars per year, a good living for those times, but much of that was eaten away by salaries for the crew, gasoline, and repairs. Her brother John captained the scow from then on. He eventually lost the *Jean K* when one December, loaded

"I've lived four lives," mused Molly. "Now, I'm softer."

with lumber and heading from Point Wolfe to Saint John, the engine exploded and destroyed the scow. The crew was rescued, but parts of the boat were found as far adrift as the waters off Nova Scotia. A record in the Canadian Registry of Shipping notes this event:

> *Jean K*, motor scow. Certificate delivered up and cancelled. Registry closed 11 January, 1946. Vessel wrecked at Delipe Cove, N.S., Dec. 14, 1945. Advice received from John Kool, owner.[9]

Molly, though childless, spent happy, productive years on land. She had married a former sailor, but they only occasionally went on voyages on other people's vessels. She was widowed some twenty years later, and began

Molly and friends sail the harbour in the wooden schooner built in her honour, St. Andrews.

work at Singer Sewing Machines in Bangor, and then, in the Dow Federal Credit Union. It was at the credit union that she met her second husband, John Carney, a businessman from Orrington, Maine.

Carney was not a natural-born sailor, but figured the fastest way to Molly's heart was through the sea. Carney wanted a saltwater boat and although he knew very little about sailing, he bought a lobster boat and had the name *Molly K* painted on the stern. "That's how he started courting me," remembers Molly. After they were married, they kept a boat for a few years. Kool was skipper and navigator as they sailed the waters of Penobscot Bay, where she used to haul freight. Even though her husband "didn't know how to tie a knot," he sailed along with her. "But I was getting old and he was getting old. And it was just too much

Kool still remembered familiar landmarks seventy years later. "I know I can't conquer the world, but there was one time when I did."

so we finally sold it. But that was fun." When she married Carney, Molly changed her citizenship, and although she became an American citizen, her affection and respect for her country of birth was always strong.

"I am an American citizen, but there's lots of things that come up, Canada versus the United States, and a lot of times I keep my mouth shut. Other times, I speak out. But no, I think anybody that lives as long in a country as I lived in Canada, and [has] respect for the country—those roots go very deep."

Molly never forgot her navigation skills and everything she had learned was useful later in her life. When she and her husband bought a fishing boat in

Rob Moore, MP (left) and Wayne Steeves, MLA (right), present a letter from Stephen Harper, Prime Minister of Canada, to Molly Kool, 2007. "I was so pleased, and so proud!"

Jonesport, Maine, she asked the seller to make sure there was plenty of oil and that the gas tanks were filled. The seller assured her that everything was just fine, but Molly's sixth sense kicked in—she checked the oil and found it was low. After this was attended to, they were ready to sail. Everything seemed to run fine. It was mid-day and the weather was cooperating. Molly knew the landmarks like the back of her hand and didn't feel the need to check the compass bearings; but it had been twenty years since Molly had made this journey, so she eventually checked the compass to make sure they were on course. The instruments said they were, but it didn't feel right to Molly.

Molly, lower left, with her siblings.

On the crossing of Ekamogan Reach, Molly was certain they were off course. She decided the compass readings were not accurate and ignored them, instead steering from memory. "So I ran for the nautical miles that was in my memory and I'm really surprised that those things would stay with you that long." She was right, of course. The compass was defective. Molly surprised her husband and on-board guests time and again. She might send someone to keep a lookout for a buoy in the fog while she was at the wheel, and would always pinpoint its location before anyone else caught sight of it. No one dared argue with "take-charge Molly."

"I guess nobody just ever argued with Molly," she said about this time. "It was one of those things. Molly was a take-charge person, you know. They laugh about me today. They say, 'Go ahead Molly. You tell us how to do it.'"

Tanning a Sail

Tanning a sail helped to prevent mildew from destroying the fabric. Acacia wood was boiled in water and the resulting mix was evaporated to produce a solution that is high in natural tannins. When immersed in this mixture, the sails were then spread on the ground to air for twenty-four hours and linseed oil was applied. Then the sails were ready.

Molly thought she might go back to sea someday, but safe harbour was where she stayed. The woman who worked "twenty-four hours and slept in what was left over," had had enough.

Sixty-four years after achieving her master's license, Molly Kool sat in her wheelchair on a deck in St. Andrews, New Brunswick, sniffing the salt air and giving great belly laughs. Gazing across the bay, she pointed out where the currents ran strongest and where the weather could get nasty.

She had just attended the christening and launch of a wooden schooner named in her honour. To the adoration of cheering crowds, she had led the sail-past of local ships. During the voyage, it was obvious she had not forgotten any of her seafaring skills, remembering all of the parts of the intricate rigging. "Bring it head to wind," she had called when a sail wouldn't come down. "They're Dacron sails," she noticed. "Back then, we had canvas and it was much heavier and of course that would come down easier. And another thing, that mast was painted." Molly referred to the old method of treating the ship's canvas by laying it down on the kitchen floor every spring to

Molly tours the harbour on the *Molly Kool*, a schooner built in her honour.

seal the air holes and paint it. "You scraped that mast and greased it and that allowed them to take the sail down with no friction."

After the celebrations, she sat basking in the afterglow.

"I went through all of it and didn't cry, but when I think about it, and all those people…" Molly had always taken things in stride, never fully realizing that she had led an extraordinary life for a woman of her time. It is no wonder, then, that she marvelled to see the crowds that had come to honour her, to touch her, to reminisce.

"In no way would I want to go back to the life that I lived then," said Molly. "It was just too hard." Molly reflected on the back-breaking nature of her work: "Today, everything's automated, but you still got to have good sense. But you've got all your navigation aids and you don't have to depend on where that tide rip is. Oh, it's almost like power steering. They can set the ship's compass. They can take a bearing on one of these radio bearings and set the ship's compass on this and just go to sleep, except for the lookout."

Molly's health was failing and Carney had already died after a long, happy marriage. Her doctor advised her that she would not be able to keep her independence. Due to vascular disease, she had lost both of her legs and was wheelchair-bound. She answered the doctor with her usual verve, her spirit once again translating into strength: "Just watch me!" She never talked about her health problems and was able to look after herself in her apartment, with daily help. Residents would see her zip through the hallways in her electric wheelchair, smiling and full of humour, her blue eyes sparkling.

She had never been a rich woman and had always watched her money. At the residence, she would play competitive games with pennies and cards with the other residents, keeping her pennies close. "Come on, come on," she would chide, "let's get all these pennies." But if another player was struggling to stay in the game, she'd be the first to throw in more of her pennies to help them out. Her fellow tenants remember her as "always telling it like it was." If something upset her, no one had to guess that something was wrong.

In her early nineties, Molly was still well enough to occasionally visit her native Alma. She would stay at an inn that offered sweeping views of the wharf and bay. Molly's Cottage, the tiny seven-by-ten-metre cedar-shingled house where she grew up, was saved from demolition and has been moved to Fundy National Park, where it is now an interpretive centre and heritage site.

"Her heart was totally here," said her friend Ken Kelly, a key player in preserving the cottage. "She'd just park her wheelchair in front of those windows and she'd be in heaven."

Back in 1992, Molly was celebrated in Alma with all the fanfare and ceremony she deserved. While military jets streaked across the sky in her honour, Molly smashed a champagne bottle over the monument bearing her name that stands at the harbourfront where the *Jean K* was built so many years ago. Later, back home in Orrington, she reminisced about that period of her life. Molly felt she was now completely different from that spirited young person who wore the captain's stripes on her coat. Time had softened her. "Well, we both have the same name," Molly Kool said of the woman she used to be, "but by now, that's about all. I feel I've lived one life as a girl growing up, one life at sea, one life with Ray, and one with John." Stroking one of her two cats, Molly reflected, "Now, I'm living even another. I'm softer. I can accept things better now. I know I can't conquer the world, but there was one time when I did.

"I think about those days, you know, but I don't know the woman I was back then," she said, sipping a rye whisky. "I'm soft now, I guess…I'm soft, but I'm still cocky. It just didn't seem like it was me who had done this. There were a lot of people there that I knew once. Their faces hadn't changed much, but their names escaped me now. It was so long ago. But I was so damned proud and so honoured.

"I've lived a lot of lives and this hasn't always been part of them, being Captain Molly Kool," she reflected. "Well, you wonder what you learned, but it sort of all came into being yesterday when so many people were almost like they worshipped me. It's an era that's ended, and I was a part of it."

The morning dawned rainy and misty, typical for the Fundy shore, but this was no ordinary day. On this day in 2009, Molly was to be given a captain's burial, her ashes scattered to the winds and waves of the Bay of Fundy. The clouds obligingly lifted and the sun burst through as Molly's surviving family members and close friends boarded the boat that would carry her remains, while the mournful lament of bagpipes drifted on the breezes. Her friends scattered her ashes to the winds and tides, the wreath was lowered, and the little boat circled the harbour buoy twice to ring the bell, returning to shore to complete the ceremony.

Dignitaries and celebrities alike attended Molly's funeral, but what might have impressed Molly most was the message sent by Commander Josée Kurtz, the first woman captain to command a Canadian warship. Molly came from a generation when women were prohibited from entering military service, but the doors had now opened with a clang that echoed through the decades.

This monument in Alma notes Molly's accomplishment: "the first woman sea captain in North America and second in the world."

Commander Kurtz was continuing the journey that Captain Kool had begun.

"Have a last safe voyage, Captain," wrote Commander Kurtz. "May the memories of you as a pioneer and leader on the sea always be as vibrant as the tides of Fundy which you so confidently navigated. I trust that our bows will cross at sea some day."

New Brunswick singer-songwriter Ruth Dunfield composed and performed this song at Molly's funeral:

MOLLY KOOL

WORDS AND MUSIC © RUTH DUNFIELD, 2003

My name is Molly Kool—I'm living off the sea
I broke uncharted waters—some say it was destiny
But I am no fool—I just do what I know best
My name is Molly Kool
My Daddy was a sea captain and he plied the Fundy coast
Though I was just a teenage girl I learned to sail anyhow
He taught me everything he knew and all the duties of a seaman
Someday I'd be the captain of his scow
My name is Molly Kool—I'm living off the sea
I broke uncharted waters—some say it was destiny
But I am no fool—I just do what I know best
My name is Molly Kool
The first thing I made sure of was I passed the mates exam
I studied navigation with the best men of the crew
It took three years to gain enough trust to give me that one chance
I became a shipmaster when I was through
My name is Molly Kool—I'm living off the sea

I broke uncharted waters– some say it was destiny
But I am no fool—I just do what I know best
My name is Molly Kool
I know that some still speak of me and my legacy lives on
They say I was a champion of the women's cause
Now that's okay—I don't mind—though it wasn't my intent
I appreciate the kind applause
My name is Molly Kool—I'm living off the sea
I broke uncharted waters—some say it was destiny
But I am no fool—I just do what I know best
My name is Molly Kool—Molly Kool[10]

Commander Josée Kurtz (left) assumed command of HMCS *Halifax* on April 6, 2009. "Don't look at yourself as a girl. Look at yourself as an individual, and bring those credentials to the table."

CHAPTER SIX
A NEW GENERATION

When Captain Molly Kool threw down the gauntlet, Commander Josée Kurtz willingly picked it up. On April 6, 2009, after twenty-three years of service, Kurtz took command of her first warship, the HMCS *Halifax*, a 4,770-tonne vessel.

"I feel great," she said during that historic moment. "I can't wait to take this ship to sea."

The first woman to command a Canadian warship, Josée Kurtz had the same yearning for adventure as Molly Kool when, as a girl in Joliette, Quebec, she heard a neighbour telling stories about his time in the military. But in 1989, at the age of eighteen, she went to the recruiting office and was encouraged to enlist. Unlike Molly, however, she did not plan to sail on a ship. By this time, a discrimination complaint with the Human Rights Commission helped to steer the Navy into allowing women to take on jobs traditionally held by male seamen. Kurtz soon earned a Master of Defence Studies from the Royal Military College of Canada, amidst other intensive training.

Kurtz acknowledges that twenty years ago, it was simply not on the radar screen for a female to command

Women in the Armed Forces

Women have been able to participate in all areas of armed combat, except in submarines, since 1989. By the year 2000, submarine warfare was open to women. There are 7,900 women serving in the Canadian Forces, a representation of 15 percent. Only 2 percent of combat troops are women, and there are ninety-nine female combat officers.

a warship and considers it a tremendous achievement to be able to demonstrate that a woman can do the job equally well. Kurtz's achievement follows on the heels of Lieutenant Commander Marta Mulkins, who, six years earlier, became commanding officer of the HMCS *Kingston*.

Kurtz admits it has not been easy. Her progress up the ladder has been demanding, first as a weapons officer, then a combat officer, and on to executive officer on the *Ville de Quebec*. Each step of the way, she has had to prove herself over and over again.

Kurtz acknowledges that she is a pioneer and, like Molly Kool, will always be alone in this achievement. Her experience parallels that of Molly, who took exams in a class full of boys, fiercely scrutinized because of her gender. Kurtz has sensed the fierce scrutiny since she entered military college in Victoria—one of a small group of women among the men. "The guys were reluctant to accept us when we women first joined, but they gradually let us do our thing. The scrutiny went away, eventually." Times had changed since Molly's era, and Kurtz was pleased that the attitude of navy personnel was to avoid

A Guiding Light

Ida Lewis (1842–1911), an American, was a lighthouse
keeper in Newport Harbour, Rhode Island. Lewis is
officially credited by the U.S. Coast Guard with at least
eighteen lifesaving rescues in the water, and likely many
more. A coast guard vessel was commissioned in her
honour in 1997. She received the Gold Lifesaving Medal
for her courage.

stereotyping and to treat both male and female cadets
equitably, but the close scrutiny was something she had
to grow accustomed to. By the time she graduated from
an advanced course, she was qualified to navigate and
took a ship out of port for the first time in her life.
The only woman among 250 men, she saw that there
were many more crewmen than usual on the bridge that
morning. "There were lots of crewmen on that deck to
watch what the navigator would do." When they saw
that she worked safely and competently, just like any
other navigator, it was business as usual and gender was
no longer an issue.

"The guys were reluctant at first," she said, "but as
long as I do my job the same as any other guy would, I
can be successful. I do not try to pull strings because I
am a woman. I put a lot of pressure on myself because
I wanted to do the job, not because I am a woman. The
navy opened the ranks and allowed us to perform. Those
who were able to do the task were promoted."

Kurtz reflected on the qualities and characteristics
that helped her to overcome the biased attitudes that
she initially encountered: "Determination, not being

Marta Mulkins, Trailblazer

Marta Mulkins, a naval officer, was promoted to Lieutenant Commander in 2001. In 2003, she was appointed commanding officer of HMCS *Kingston*, a military warship with a crew of forty-three. Lieutenant Commander Mulkin won an award in 2004 as one of Canada's Most Powerful Women, in the Trailblazer category, representing women who are first in their fields.

over-sensitive, an acute sense of awareness of those issues, not wanting to be a guy but understanding the guys, and being able to diplomatically discuss with them on the basis of competency." She feels she has achieved her goals—she has shown that women can do the job on the basis of competence and not gender. "The guys have never made me feel otherwise…I've never felt like they were looking at me as a girl but as a colleague."

Kurtz acknowledges Molly Kool's role in creating a place for women in a male-dominated environment. She knows that it has now fallen on her shoulders to make a place for women on warships, a place that has been dominated by men for hundreds of years. She knows that it will require some give and take from the male seamen so that she, and women like her, can create this place for themselves.

Like Molly Kool before her, Commander Kurtz has followed her passion. When the navy first opened its doors to women, Kurtz, one of ten women, was the only one in her group to advance. This is gradually changing as more women in training see others alongside them.

Victoria Drummond

Victoria Drummond (1896–1978) born in Norfolk, England, was the first British woman to serve as chief engineer in World War Two. She received the Lloyd's War Medal for bravery at sea for keeping her ship's engines running after it was disabled by an enemy bomb.

Kurtz believes the only drawback in a career for seafaring women is the consideration of home and family. Long absences from home mean many sacrifices on the part of a woman's family. The influx of women aboard ships has created a necessity for maternity leave. The navy has extended these benefits to the men, so their lives have improved as a result of the presence of women. Men can now take five weeks of paternity leave, a benefit that wasn't considered or granted until women came on board.

Kurtz is happy to serve as a positive role model to the eighteen women who serve on her ship, and to those women new to the forces. "I do realize, however, that because of what I am and because of my place in time, my position is significant to many women. They look up to what I have done."

Molly Kool hauled gravel, pumped the bilge, and performed as best she could. She was annoyed when she couldn't do the heavy work that a man could do. Molly used to navigate using a compass and the stars, but today's electronic equipment eliminates the need for much of the guesswork and instinct she relied upon, and Kurtz is not confronted with demands to perform work requiring physical strength. However, like Molly,

The HMCS *Halifax* is a modern warship with a crew of 225, named after the city of Halifax and built by Saint John Shipbuilding Ltd.

Kurtz finds work in a moving environment that is always changing physically taxing for both men and women. And just as Molly Kool cooked for her crew, Kurtz can occasionally be found flipping eggs in the galley.

"There are many satisfying moments," she says, describing how she enjoys cooking breakfast for her crew on Sunday mornings. "Small conversations go a long way with the sailors."

Kurtz does differ from Molly in one way—her ongoing struggle with seasickness. Molly was seasick for the first and

An Impressive Ship

HMCS *Halifax* is one of the most advanced warships in the world. It carries anti-submarine, anti-surface, and anti-air warfare. Built in Saint John, New Brunswick, it is the second Canadian warship to be named after the city of Halifax, Nova Scotia.

only time when she was five years old on board the *Jean K.* The first time Kurtz was on board a ship, she had a similar experience. "On my first day at sea, we were a couple of miles out, I turned green pretty quick with the swell. I stared at the horizon hoping it would go away." Unlike Molly, Kurtz never got over her tendency to seasickness, and in a job that requires extreme focus, this could be a serious setback. Medications help her during voyages and prevent this miserable affliction from hindering her ability to work.

Kurtz takes responsibility for setting the tone for a comfortable and respectful work atmosphere on the ship. Part of this responsibility requires the ability to keep open lines of communication. "If I can show them that I am also working within the same constraints as they are below deck, that's the message I like to send," she says. Kurtz has a crew of 206 with eighteen women serving at all levels, from ordinary seaman to lieutenant navy. The highest-ranking woman on board is the commander herself.

Kurtz feels there is no limit to the ways she and other women can serve in the navy. As women and men move up the ranks, career progression becomes competitive. Kurtz knows that if she is promoted, it will be because she has demonstrated her competency as

Mary Patten in Command

Mary Patten (1837–61), an American, was the only woman to take command of a clipper ship. This occurred in 1857 in a voyage from San Fransisco to New York around Cape Horn. When the captain, Patten's husband, fell seriously ill, Mary Patten, only twenty-one, and an expert in navigation, took command. She was pregnant at the time.

a commander, and that gender will not be a deciding factor in her progression. "We've all made it to a level where we demonstrate that we're good at what we do; positions become fewer and farther between. I have the ambition to move up, I have something else to offer, but I have to demonstrate my competency. The Admiralty and superior officers will look at me among all my peers and determine where I will be employed next. They will treat me equally."

The long hours of work are outweighed by the lasting friendships, the travel and training opportunities, and the life-changing experiences. For example, Kurtz spent two months giving aid to the victims of the 2010 earthquake in Haiti, a life-changing experience she will always remember. In port, she and her crew are never idle as they prepare, for the next deployment or as a "ready-duty" ship, ready at eight hours notice to respond to any contingency. "There is always one ship, on a rotation basis," says Kurtz. Each year, HMCS *Halifax* and other naval vessels are open to the public, including school children. Lucky children might try on firefighting gear and push buttons in the operations room. Kurtz's hus-

Molly reminisces in Alma, 1992.

band was in the navy for twenty years and is now at home taking care of their young daughter. Kurtz maintains that without her husband, she would not be where she is today. She says that although the navy offers unlimited opportunities, there are long months away from home and this places demands on her family, especially her young daughter. "She understands that her mother's career is important, both to me and in terms of what the military does in Canada, and for Canada and abroad," she says. "She's just not that keen on sharing her mom with the sea and with the military." Despite having a mother who is a naval commander and a father who is a retired naval officer, Kurtz's daughter has no interest in pursuing a career in the navy. When she asks her mother if she can be anything she wants to be when she grows up, Kurtz, the supreme role model, answers with a resounding "yes." If you listen carefully, you can hear the hint of an echo in that answer. An echo, because the words, the deeds, the accomplishments, and the raw grit of Captain Molly Kool paved the way and made possible these brand new opportunities for women.

Molly Kool and the line of women pioneers before her ultimately cleared the path to limitless opportunities. Says Commander Josée Kurtz to young Canadian women considering a career in the navy, or indeed, in any male-dominated field: "Just go for it—but be prepared to demonstrate that you can not only talk the talk, but walk the walk. In a demanding environment, don't look at yourself as a girl, look at yourself as an individual with credentials and bring those credentials to the table. Can you do anything? Absolutely!"

Captain Molly Kool, the woman who fired the imaginations of three generations of women, who sailed in any weather condition, through whirlpools, rapids, and high winds, was rarely afraid to take the wheel. Whenever she faltered, she remembered her father and how she would ask him, "Dad, do you want to take the wheel?" He would invariably reply, "No, Molly. Go ahead, girl. You can do it." When all is said and done, this is the true legacy of a bold woman who saw only possibilities where others saw limitations. If Molly were alive today, no doubt these are the very same words she would offer to any young woman about to embark on a groundbreaking, or gender-defying, career.

"Go ahead, girl. You can do it!"

ACKNOWLEDGEMENTS

My sincere thanks go to Joni-Anne Carlisle for her enthusiastic support in offering her reminiscences and images, to Fred Farrell, curator, who patiently guided me through the Molly Kool archival collection at the Archives of New Brunswick, to Josée Kurtz, Commanding Officer, HMCS *Halifax,* for generously giving her time to talk of her experiences, and Major Paul Doucette for helping to make it happen. Thanks also to Donald Alward, Robert Appel, Cheryl Barr, Charlie Campo, Ruth Dunfield (ruthdunfield.com), Rita Hopper, Angela Johnson, Ken Kelly, Mary Majka, Sheena Mason, Ed Meyer, Hon. Rob Moore, MP Fundy Royal, Mayor Hillyard Rossiter, Hirta Short, my tireless editor Patrick Murphy, and finally, to research librarians everywhere.

NOTES

All Molly Kool's quotes, unless otherwise noted, are taken from a collection of interviews and speeches at the Provincial Archives of New Brunswick (see bibliography)

1. *Mirror of the Sea*; Conrad, Joseph, 1906

2. *Gender and History in Canada*; Parr, Joy. Copp Clark, 1996, p. 257

3. ibid, p. 256

4. *Chocolate River: A Story of the Petitcodiac River*; Larracey, E., 1985, p. 186

5. *1918–1939 Canadian Women: A History*; Prentice, Alison, 1996, p. 249

6. *Chocolate River*; Larracey, E., p. 194

7. Department of Justice, Canada; Marine Personnel Regulations

8. ©Ripley's Entertainment Inc.

9. *Framing Our Past: Canadian Women's History in the 20th Century*; Cook, Sharon, 2001, p. 185

10. *Chocolate River*; Larracey, E. 1985, p. 190

11. Copyright 2003 Ruth Dunfield (ruthdunfield.com)

BIBLIOGRAPHY

Anson, P. *Fisher Folklore: Old Customs, taboos and superstitions among fisher folk.* London: Faith Press, 1965.

Baird, Donald. *Women at Sea in the Age of Sail.* Halifax: Nimbus, 2001.

Beckett, W. *A Few Naval Customs, Expressions, Traditions and Superstitions.* Portsmouth: Gieves, Ltd., 1931.

Benoit, Cecilia. *Women, Work, and Social Rights: Canada in historical and comparative perspective.* Scarborough: Prentice Hall, 2000.

Blaney, Harold A. *The Way It Was Back Then: Grampy Remembers: A collection of stories.* Millville, NB, c1990.

Broadfoot, Barry. *Ten Lost Years, 1929–1939: Memories of Canadians Who Survived the Depression,* Toronto: Doubleday, 1973.

Carr, Frank G. *Sailing Barges.* London: P. Davies, 1951.

Cook, S. A. et al. *Framing Our Past: Canadian Women's History in the Twentieth Century.* Montreal: McGill-Queen's University Press, 2001.

Larracey, E. *Chocolate River: A Story of the Petitcodiac River from the beginning of the habitation in the late 1600s until the building of the causeway at Moncton.* Hantsport NS: Lancelot Press, 1985.

Leacock, Stephen et al. *Canada's War at Sea,* Montreal: Alvah M. Beatty Publications Ltd., 1944.

McKee, Fraser M. *Sink All the Shipping There: the Wartime Loss of Canada's Merchant Ships and Fishing Schooners.*
St. Catherine's, ON: Vanwell Publishing, 2004.

Mennill, Paul. *The Depression Years: Canada in the 1930s.* Scarborough: Prentice-Hall, 1978.

Nemiroff, Greta H., ed. *Women's Changing Landscapes: Life Stories from Three Generations.* Toronto: Second Story Press, 1999.

Parr, J. and M. Rosenfeld. *Gender and History in Canada.* Copp Clark, 1996.

Prentice, A. *1918-1939 Canadian Women, a history.* Copp Clark, 1996.

Provincial Archives of New Brunswick: Molly Kool interviews MC1363, MS2; MS3; MS4; MS5; P471.

Sager, Eric. *Ships and Memories: Merchant Seafarers in Canada's Age of Steam.* Vancouver: UBC Press, 1993.

Zarema, E. *The Privilege of Sex: A Century of Canadian Women,* Toronto: Anansi, 1974.

IMAGE CREDITS

INDEX

STORIES OF
OUR PAST